PAULINA PANTYLEVA

My Secret Life as a Sex Addict

How I Repaired the Damage

PLATYPUS

PUBLISHING

This book is dedicated to my husband, Richard, whom I love with all my heart. He suffered due to my sex addiction as well. Yet, he was able to distinguish me from the addiction itself and for that, I am eternally grateful.

Epigraph

<u>Kintsugi Vase</u>

When a ceramic bowl breaks into pieces, we often see it as garbage.

In Japanese art, potential beauty is seen in reconstructing the broken pieces. The pieces are held together with gold lacquer. The more repair that has been done, the more valuable the vase.

It is the imperfections that make it more beautiful.

That is my cover art.

That is me.

Contents

III   My Recovery

Foreword

By Dana Lee Chapman

When the world feels like it's just too much to handle, humans will find all sorts of ways to escape the overwhelm. For my client Paulina, the author of this book, sex and food became the go-to ways to get through the harsh pressures, responsibilities and realities of life.

Sex can provide a sense of love, satisfaction, gratification, nourishment, connection and indulgence. So can food.

Food can fill an empty hole. So can sex.

Until they can't.

My name is Dana Lee Chapman and although I am known as The Diet Recovery Coach who helps women heal from the collateral damage of diet culture, including food dysfunction and body image issues, the heart of what I do with my clients is repair the relationship they have with themselves, regardless of the affliction or addiction.

After nearly 30 years of working with women who have dysfunctional coping mechanisms, the number one thing that has made the greatest and most profound impact in their lives is their willingness to deconstruct and then reconstruct what it means to truly love themselves, making Paulina's artwork you see on the cover an ideal and beautiful representation of this entire fragmented process.

Paulina and I met a few short months after one of the most painful events in her life which brought on binge eating episodes like never before.

The event is something she writes about in a later section of this book. It is a pivotal point in her own journey when she fell to the depths of what, she later learned, was required to turn her life around. The fact that she can even write about it in such an insightful and reflective manner is a testament to how far she has come on her path to recovering from both sex addiction and food addiction in such a short amount of time.

It took her roughly a year from "decision day" when we began our work together to when she completed the writing of this book. When you are *in it* and are experiencing excruciating emotional pain just wanting to "be on the other side of the recovery already!" it may seem like a year is a long time to take to turn things around.

However, a part of what made the transformation possible is the approach. I encouraged her to go slower than she's ever been willing to go because if she paced herself, she would experience more effective and permanent change. Although she was anxious and rushed through our work in the beginning, she did see the value in switching gears and eventually gave this approach a shot.

Healing will take as long as it takes. While you can use a pivotal event as the catalyst to make a decisive change, the more gradual, introspective, and mindful you are after that commitment to yourself, the more accelerated and lasting the impact.

As Paulina discovered through our work together, it's not about the FOOD and, that quickly translated to mean it must not be about the SEX either. As it turns out (spoiler alert), these are just the placeholders that symbolized her innermost beliefs regarding self-worth and her value in this world.

An unfortunate truth is that sex addiction in our society and our culture is far more acceptable and prevalent to discuss in regard to men than women. Paulina and I both agree that needs to change.

Because our work together helped Paulina uncover a deeper understanding as to why she did the things she did, she made a decision that none of it would go to waste. Sharing the real, raw truth of a woman with a sex addiction is an opportunity to help other women along with their partners, family and friends, who are suffering in silence find some peace and some answers.

When a person can feel validated and less ashamed of their secrets, an ease of relief sets in. May this book shed light, insight, and warmth on some of the darkness and give you hope that no matter how many years this has haunted you, you too have the possibility of healing and recovery at the point you decide you are good and ready.

Whether you are someone who has full awareness of your sex addiction and are at the point of admitting it, or you are currently swirling in feelings and ideas trying to figure out if this sex thing is an actual problem with a name, whichever the case may be, it's a really good sign that you have been drawn to this book. Reading about sex addiction from the woman's perspective might help you see your experiences from a more reality-based view so that you too can uncover patterns and find answers to determine where to go from here.

If you are someone who picked this book up to better understand the behavior of the one you love or deeply care about, or to learn more about this addiction out of curiosity, I commend you. It's an incredible thing to do as a human - to seek to understand why those we love do the things they do. Especially when it can be so destructive and hurtful and make no sense from the outside looking in.

The truth is, even from first person perspective, gaining insight is extremely complicated and layered, which is why addiction is so compulsive and repetitive. It's a trauma response and that response does not involve logic.

The other extremely important thing to consider is that most people are afraid to do the work to learn about themselves for fear that it will stir up painful emotions from the past. However, this will lead to unraveling that messy web of answers. That becomes more of what I began this foreword with: When the world feels like it's just too much to handle, humans will find all sorts of ways to escape the overwhelm. It becomes a vicious cycle until compassion, patience, and understanding can embody all persons involved in order to move forward in the healthiest, most sustainable way possible.

All of life's events have a purpose and meaning, even if it is difficult to see the "why" in the moment. Hopefully, this book can allow you to gain a greater perspective of the events in your life that have caused harmful coping behaviors. A more compassionate view can allow you to create a clear picture from which damaged relationships have a chance to mend, be deepened and even enriched to a level you never thought possible.

Paulina shares, openly and honestly, stories of how her addictions revealed themselves in the sneakiest of ways throughout her life. The stories demonstrate her learning lessons. Those lessons are here to be discovered as a mirror to your own life circumstances, should you be open to that next step for yourself. Paulina poses some rhetorical questions for her readers, but my invitation to you is to not just skim past them, but to take the opportunity to really contemplate.

Dana Lee Chapman
Creator of The RealFit Mindset Course & The MindFit Method
Website: www.RealFit.tv

I

Does Sex Addiction Really Exist?

1

Hard Earned Wisdom

I have sucked a lot of cock to earn my hard-earned wisdom. I don't owe my wisdom to anybody, but it would be nice if something good came out of all the cock-sucking.

Mostly, I am doing this for me, to make ultimate sense of everything that has happened. And it has worked. I am remarkably more peaceful after writing this book. It is evident now that what I viewed as a series of unfortunate events, actually had a reason, an order, and a purpose.

I still have a fear that some pussy-faced motherfucker is going to read this book and recognize me, or with all the technology that exists, a determined self-righteous son-of-a bitch could figure out who I am and out me.

By writing this book, I have exposed the secrets in my life and therefore ruined my own reputation. I am now free to be my authentic self.

However, my kids and husband have already suffered through my addiction privately and I don't want them to go through it again publicly, and hear all about my cock-sucking.

The past few years I have taken stock of my issues and really cleaned my shit up. So if you are a sanctimonious limp-dick and looking to judge me harshly, I say, take stock of your own shit first. You know what they say about people in glass houses.

I have learned many beneficial insights from others who make themselves vulnerable and have revealed their weaknesses, fears, and failures. Now it's my turn to contribute all of the above in order to help that one person heal and recover.

Important to Note: Impotence is a medical problem that carries no judgment. "Limp-dick" is meant to be a slur and it is also non-gendered.

All the names in this book have been changed to protect the privacy of the individual except for Coach Dana.

2

Decades of Dysfunction

Therapists I had seen earlier in my life were not able to fundamentally help me. At age 49 I was depressed (again), overweight and eating out of control, and experiencing health consequences of high blood pressure and high cholesterol. I had gained 30 pounds in 4 months, again.

I felt anger, sadness, resentment, and a lack of control. I was grasping at whatever straws I could with self-help books, and following social media fitness coaches. Nobody resonated with me.

I needed to improve my situation before I hit the 50-year milestone. I did not want to hit this important milestone still a mess. I came across Dana Lee Chapman, a mindset coach who specialized in helping women overcome disordered eating.

I technically hired her as my Diet Recovery Coach, but our work together allowed me to overcome my sex addiction as well.

3

Am I The Only One?

This topic is obviously shameful because as of now, there are less than a handful of female sex addicts writing from a first-hand sex addiction experience on most search engines. The statistics on sex addiction are that 95% of people afflicted are male, half of them white, and most of them affluent and religious. Perhaps they are a different variety of sex addict born out of extreme repression. Perhaps this is the sex addict demographic that gets caught or seeks treatment, and is therefore more visible. My suspicion is that this statistic and stereotype is highly inaccurate and that many more women are affected but they have never been identified as such.

There are numerous books from a first-hand male perspective. There are some books with a wife's perspective. There are some therapists writing about their patients.

But, there are very few female heterosexual women writing in first person, as the sexaholic. And while there are similarities in regard to childhood trauma, our stories are quite varied.

I am age 50 at the time of writing this book. I am a mother to adult children and I work as a physician, but not as a mental health professional.

Often the female sex addict is judged and misunderstood to be the desperate, slutty girl, or the home wrecker. Is she the chick with too much makeup and her tits hanging out sitting at the bar? Is she the drunk friend that hits on your husband?

I never hung out at bars. I drank little alcohol and did not use drugs. I had a clean cut look. I wasn't an "obvious addict" like a crystal meth-head shuffling on the sidewalk, in baggy clothes, with her teeth rotted out. Yet, my addiction was no less destructive. I was superficially cheerful and high functioning. I played the mom role at parent-teacher conferences, and did well at my job. It would be difficult to imagine that I would suck a stranger's cock kneeling on a public bathroom floor.

You are much more likely to come across the female sex addict in her "real life" as a white collar professional or soccer mom, and never suspect what she does in her "secret life." The lack of a "look" makes it that much more secretive.

I have met several female sex addicts in my life. The interesting thing is that they were completely unaware that they were sex addicts. Just like I was unaware until the age of 35!

4

"This Is Just An Excuse To Cheat"

Sex addiction is misunderstood. People unfamiliar with it may have preconceived notions about the term meaning the frequency, length of time spent in actual intercourse or similarly simplistic view of the physical nature of sex.

The Merriam-Webster dictionary states that the first known use of the term "nymphomaniac" was in 1828. It was used to describe a cat with excessive sexual desire brought on by hormone imbalance. Somehow the term evolved to describe a woman with excessive sexual desire. If you break down the word; nymph- 1. A mythological spirit of nature imagined as a beautiful maiden inhabiting rivers, woods, or other locations 2. An immature form of an insect. Maniac- You understand. Some people still use the term nymphomaniac, likely imagining a woman in the throes of prolonged orgasm and ecstatic love-making. I am neither a nymph or a maniac. I am not a cat with a hormone imbalance. This is definitely an outdated term and inaccurate.

Oddly, the term sex addict does not exist in the Merriam-Webster dictionary. If you enter "sex addict definition" in a search engine, you will get websites with checklists of what does and does not define sex addiction.

In actuality, much less of sex addiction is the actual physical part of genital contact. It is much more complex, as I explain further.

5

What Is Sex Addiction?

Addiction likes to play mind tricks convincing you that your behavior is a choice rather than a compulsion. Addiction makes you think that you are in control when you are not. Addiction makes you think that what you are doing is just a "good time" and all for fun.

I used to think my sexual escapades or food binges were just innocent enjoyment. I deserved a little bit of pleasure in my stressful life. It's not like I was doing heroin in some alley or drinking to oblivion.

It wasn't until I was crying, distraught, begging for my husband to take me back for weeks on end that I realized that I had a problem. I made promises to myself and to my husband, Richard, that I would stop my perilous behaviors, but I continued to relapse.

Gabor Maté MD is a family physician who specializes in addiction medicine. He wrote a profoundly impactful book called *In the*

Realm of Hungry Ghosts. This book is the basis for much of my knowledge on addiction and a tool for my recovery. I like Maté's definition of the term Addiction. I use it repeatedly in this book to convey how I fit this definition.

"Addiction is any repeated behavior, substance-related or not, in which a person feels compelled to persist, regardless of its negative impact on his life and the lives of others. Addiction involves:

1. compulsive engagement with the behavior, preoccupation with it
2. impaired control over the behavior
3. persistence or relapse despite evidence of harm
4. dissatisfaction, irritability, or intense craving when the activity is not immediately available.

Compulsion, impaired control, persistence, irritability, relapse, and craving- these are the hallmarks of addiction, any addiction."

With this definition, a person can be addicted to anything.

Dr. Maté himself, states he was addicted to work and to collecting classical music CDs.

He was addicted to work because it gave him a sense of importance that he craved as a child. He collected classical music CDs because he genuinely loved music, but it was to the detriment of his finances, responsibilities, and relationships.

It may be difficult to relate to another person's specific addiction. For this reason, one might deny the possibility of its existence. For example, when Dr. Maté states that he is addicted to his work or buying CDs, at face value, it may be difficult for me to imagine such a thing. Likewise, someone who does not suffer from sex addiction might think that it's just a made-up term to make an excuse for cheating.

The good news is that it is not your job to convince anyone. The only thing that matters is that you acknowledge your sex addiction so you can overcome it.

6

It's Not About The Sex

Sex addiction is a misnomer because it's not about sex itself. That is a typical myth that many people believe. The sex, in actuality, is disappointing and ultimately makes you worry about your health while it diminishes your self-esteem.

Furthermore, it's not about being unhappy with your significant other. Countless times, I explained that to my husband, Richard. It was a very difficult concept to understand. It was about my emotional deficits, not deficits in our relationship.

If I had to rename the term sex addiction, I would call it "Fantasy Addiction" or even "Addiction to Fairy Tales." I escaped my real-life problems with compulsive fantasies of romanticized sexual experiences.

My life was hard and a struggle and I needed an escape. It was much more pleasant to live in the fantasy world of hot, seductive, connected sex.

I used to think about sex most of my waking hours. I would be distracted by my fantasies, sexting, and searching for online hookups. It was my way of coping with my typical stressful life, day-to-day problems, and rat race.

I would have been so much more productive if my time and energy was spent on what I was actually supposed to be doing. In reality, my sex encounters were a constant stream of disappointment followed by guilt and consequences.

For now, I will just stick to the somewhat inaccurate term, sex addiction, for the purposes of this book.

II

Overdosing on Sex

7

Sex For Trade At A Young Age

In my research for this book, I saw a statistic that 100% of sex addicts (and likely any type of addict) were either sexually abused as children, physically abused, or emotionally abused. This is how my sex addiction started.

When I was eight years old I would often go to my best friend's house. I was a child of immigrant parents who worked a lot, and therefore I was often unsupervised.

My friend had a 12-year-old brother, Johnny, who was a bit of a scummy pre-teen. I didn't think he was scummy at the time. I thought he was cool and older, and fun.

Johnny liked to coerce me to go into his garage fort or his bedroom and we would make out and he would dry hump me and feel my boobs. I was an early bloomer and started to get breasts at age 8. By age 11, I was a full C cup.

Note that I didn't say I was sexually abused. I always thought I was a fully consensual participant in this sexual behavior and that no abuse had occurred. I don't like victim mentality so this chapter is about how my sex addiction originated. It is an explanation and not an excuse, and prefer not to have it come across as a victim statement.

I had undergone "grooming," which means that my abuser gained my favor and participation by pretending to be my friend and to convince me that we had a special relationship that was secretive, fun, and special. This is a common strategy of child abusers to decrease the risk of getting caught. That is why I always thought that I enjoyed it and participated in it willingly.

I would make out with him and allow him to fondle me in exchange for cigarettes.

I liked to smoke at age 8. I always felt that the sexual behavior was consensual and that I enjoyed it, participated in it, and possibly encouraged it to happen.

In retrospect, not that I think an 8-year-old could consent to a 12-year-old, but it wasn't violent or mean, or brutal. It was kind of fun and a turn-on at that time. But, I knew that it was not acceptable to my parents or society and therefore needed to be kept secret.

This non-penetrative type of heavy petting and titty-sucking in exchange for cigarettes continued until I was 11 years old.

This was the 1980s when kids could get cigarettes out of a vending machine or say you were buying them for your parents.

It's situations like me and Johnny that created the helicopter parent movement. I was still in the free-range child era which had its benefits and drawbacks.

Then my mom discovered a hickey on my breast and asked me if Johnny was touching me. I vehemently denied it and said it was a bruise from an injury. I was too ashamed to admit the truth, but my mom was right to be suspicious of Johnny and wouldn't let me go to my friend's house and that is how our friendship dissolved.

I didn't consciously view the Johnny experience as traumatic, but apparently my subconscious mind did. I have since learned that what I had was a discordant reaction. This means that although I knew what was happening was wrong, my body reacted with pleasure because I was being sexually stimulated. This discordant reaction really messed with my mind from that point onward. I now associated doing something "wrong" with pleasure. As a result, I felt shame and guilt for feeling this way. The shame and guilt made me crave an escape to this feeling. The activity I chose as an "escape" created more shame and guilt. A catch 22 was created.

From the Johnny experience onward, I was the kid that liked to make out if we were playing hide and seek and was often looking for make-out sessions with random teen boys on the beach or on vacations. I became sex obsessed.

Oddly, I did not have any continuing interest in smoking cigarettes.

At age 11 when the Johnny-sex ended, I have my first memory of secretly binge eating. I have since learned that food and sex addiction are a common duality. Perhaps it is playing a role in the current obesity epidemic.

As a teen and young adult, I was the promiscuous girl always chasing the boys. I liked Hustler and Penthouse more than Playboy magazines because they were more explicit. I had been exposed to porn since age 8 from finding my father's stash of magazines. I had also seen the butt rape scene from the movie "Last tango in Paris," at age 12, watching cable t.v. at the house where I babysat late at night. It had become forever etched in my mind as a "trauma" and something that fascinated me. I would need to relive that scene in my future. That is how trauma often works.

Although I was always a good student and didn't get into any type of trouble, my mother had a difficult time with me on vacations because I was always sneaking away with a boy.

I was the Spring break slut during college. I was generally sex obsessed, but it blended in as normal at that time.

For the most part it was still generally fun. My slutty behavior continued until my marriage to my first husband, my college sweetheart, at the young age of 22.

From my teens and into adulthood, I had a sexual preference for molestation-type of sexual experiences. I had a predilection to role-play or to relive the molestation I underwent as a child.

I would enjoy laying really still and quiet while a more dominant man, slowly, gently works his way with his hand over my body, my breasts, and thighs, then slips his hands closer to my vagina, parting my legs.

I would pretend that I don't like it and that this is all wrong to do, but I couldn't deny how tremendously turned on I would get. It formed my sexual taste as a Submissive. When I would act out on my sex addiction as an adult, it seems I was always searching for the ultimate submissive experience.

I think it is peculiar that my childhood experience stuck with me throughout my entire life and shaped my sexual preferences so intensely. It makes sense, but it's still quite shocking how much our childhood experiences mold us.

Childhood sex abuse can result in hyper-sexualization like in my case, or hypo-sexualization, where a person wants nothing to do with sex.

I am in my 50's now and these sexual preferences are still with me, but to do with my husband only.

My childhood experiences are insights into my psyche. Few people leave childhood unscathed. Whatever the bad or weird things that happened to me in childhood, I now allow them to provide insight and not become a life sentence of punishment for myself.

What were some childhood and teen memories that you have that formed your tastes, likes, dislikes, and attitudes toward sex?

Were any of these memories traumatic in the sense that they were extremely formative due to the potency of the feeling or memory?

Do you recreate or gravitate toward similar sexual experiences like the ones that traumatized you as a child?

A note about Johnny. Johnny was aged 12 to 15 years during his sexual grooming of me. If this had been today and reported, Johnny would go to jail as a sex offender and his life would be ruined forever. Is that what his punishment should be? I don't think so. He was just a child himself, doing what he did as an unsupervised, horney teenage boy. Author and social media personality Joshua T. Berglan made a 2023 docuseries entitled "The Juveniles of MSOP" which is a civil containment center for sex-offending youth. While it is not called a prison, it has the same type of conditions and has softer requirements for keeping a person locked indefinitely. The docuseries chronicles the spiral of incarceration and ruined lives when this type of soft crime is mishandled in underage perpetrators. They are more victims than abusers, in my opinion. It is good to see the perspective of the youth sex offender in these types of situations because it demonstrates that they are a victim as well.

8

My Great Escape

L ife was stressful. I know someone always has it tougher than me, and yet I still want to acknowledge that I felt debilitating stress at several pivotal points in my life that made me want to self-medicate with my sex and food addictions.

At age 25, I gave birth to triplets, two boys and a girl. My first husband and I moved into my parent's house. We needed help financially and with childcare.

While my parents are wonderful, it was tight quarters with little privacy, and too much baby stress. Since the babies were significantly premature at 28 weeks, they had medical issues in the first year of life.

Alex, the child who is permanently disabled, had more than his fair share of hardships. He is the million-dollar (at minimum) child. We did every type of therapy that existed to optimize him and to get him to walk.

It was a full-time job just to go to his doctor's appointments and therapies, and to help with bathing, dressing, and grooming past the age any child could do it on his own.

Additionally, there were multiple difficult surgeries, hospital admissions, and all the emotional stress that comes with that.

I felt despair while experiencing multiple medical crises related to Alex over the course of many years.

I had to work extremely long hours to support the kids, pay for nannies, activities, all the usual stuff related to kids, medical bills, and there was constant financial stress and emotional fatigue.

I juggled opening my medical practice while still working long hours in the Emergency Room.

My first husband and I divorced after 5 years of marriage, partly because of my sex addiction, but more so due to other factors.

I underwent a stressful IRS audit and had extortion-level accounting fees. There were other problems that are still too upsetting to even write about.

I had anger and resentment over issues relating to Alex's education, feelings of abandonment by my husband, sadness, anger relating to various government agencies, bureaucracy, and overall unfairness of life and the world.

It was really hard, and still is, being a mom to a disabled child. There is endless bureaucracy and unfairness in obtaining help and resources.

I was a busy, working mom, juggling too many things. I felt chronically fatigued and overwhelmed. And there was no anti-depressant, no anxiolytic, no psychotherapist, that could alleviate the chronic stress and PTSD related to constant medical crisis's.

Sex addiction was my great escape.

I binged excessively on my sex addiction in the two years after my divorce and until I entered a serious relationship with my second (and current) husband, Richard.

9

Like a Dog In Heat

F itness and being slim were always important to me. When I dieted, always in a very unhealthy manner, but was slim and fit, I would want reinforcement by looking attractive to men.

The sex behaviors would fuel the endorphin high and would lessen my appetite. When I would feel disappointed and ashamed of my sexual behavior, I would comfort myself with junk food.

The junk foods would create weight gain, make me feel worse about myself, and make me eat more or crave a sexual escapade to thrill me.

After my divorce, at age 27, I went on a 5-day cruise with two girlfriends. I was looking and feeling good and it was my first vacation as a single lady in 5 years.

Have you ever seen a dog in heat? They writhe around on

the ground or present their ass to you, even though you're not another dog to fuck them? They look at you with their moon eyes like, " I wuvvvv youuuuu."

That was me.

I was a desperate dog in heat and if a man had a penis, that was my one and only requirement to fuck. Got penis? Will fuck. It might as well have been written on my forehead.

I got what I wanted. I fucked seven men in 5 days. I made out with a few more. And I ate a whole lot of ship food.

The two girlfriends I went on the cruise with, didn't want to be my friends after this vacation. Go figure.

It was the fourth day of the cruise and I was already on my seventh penis. I met Jack at the pizza station by the pool.

I went there to binge on pizza, partly because pizza is delicious, and partly to punish my bad behaviors with food. I just wanted to engorge myself with cheese, crust, soda, and more cheese like a bloated tick.

Jack says to me "Hey, I've been seeing you around. This pizza isn't the greatest..." blah blah blah, a few minutes of small talk...Next thing I know, I'm on my knees in the closest men's bathroom to the pizza station. No kissing, no foreplay, just cock in mouth, suck suck suck squirt.

Jack finishes with, "Thank you so much. I needed that so

badly. I was going crazy hanging out with my wife and kids this entire cruise. I gotta go…"

At the time, I didn't know how I would find myself in these kinds of situations. It seemed to only happen to me. Somehow I attract random men to do this. I don't even like to suck cock. Much less, a guy I don't even know, who has a wife and kids. Cock is disgusting so why did I suck it?! What the fuck is wrong with me?

Now in hindsight, when I try to make sense of this behavior I think there are two possibilities. Perhaps I craved misdirected self-validation and a dose of self-esteem that someone was attracted to me. Or perhaps I was seeking punishment. *Or both.*

Jack provided that with his small talk and momentary attention to me. He "saw me around."

That was actually a beautiful compliment to me. It gave me a thrill and somehow made me feel better about myself…better until I was gargling water and hand soap, trying to get his penis stench off my oral membranes, kicking myself for being such a whore, feeling punished.

And that's an insult to whores because I didn't even get paid for that. Actually, I was the one who paid. I further damaged my self-esteem and self-worth.

Dear Forgiving God, thank you for sparing me from any STDs. The health risks I disregarded were tremendous.

10

For a Smart Person, I Did Really Dumb Things

I f there's only one take-away from this book, this is it. Never put a beer bottle up your snatch. It will give you a raging yeast infection and you will have cottage cheese curd pouring out of your pussy hole and you will be racing to the doctor to cure you of this hideous malady.

I know this from personal experience.

After my divorce and before I met Richard, I dated this guy, Todd, that I was not into at all. A recurring theme- I hung out with a lot of men that I was not into because it still fed my self-esteem that someone, anyone, was interested in me.

I was at his house and he was watching football, which I have no interest in, and he was drinking a bottle of beer and eating chicken wings and I was really bored, and (I thought) I wanted sex. He finished his beer and he had no interest in sex and he couldn't get it up so I was like,

"Hey baby, fuck me with that nice long beer bottle."

So he did.

Fast forward to the following day. Itchy, gushing, red, swollen, vagina, and labia on fire. I needed *fluconazole* asap.

I was smart enough to get a medical degree, but I have done the dumbest, most stupid, utterly ridiculous things in my life.

11

Some Things Are Still Hard To Explain

After the beer bottle incident with Todd, his friends came over that night to watch football. I was still bored and started making eyes at Frank. Frank and I start to make out in front of eight or so guys in the living room. My shirt comes off and I'm on the floor with my legs wrapped around Frank and it's a total show. I start sucking his cock right there in front of everybody.

Now mind you, I hate sucking cock, but there was an audience, so it made it more extreme, and therefore more fun and worth it.

The other guys are like, "Hey can I get some of that too?" I go over to some other guy and suck his cock. Then I get a request for another. Free blowjobs! What a find. The other guys wanted a little bit of privacy so I went to a bedroom and sucked a few more guys one by one.

You know that scene in the movie Forrest Gump, where Forrest runs across the country and then turns around and runs back across the country again, and it was after Jenny left him, and he wasn't running for any particular reason that he could explain? Journalists were running after him asking why he was running and he answered, "I just felt like running."

That was me with my cock sucking marathon. I didn't know why I was doing that at the moment. I was just running. It's still hard to explain why even 23 years later.

The day after my marathon, I got a vaginal yeast infection because of the beer bottle incident. At this point, I felt at my lowest. I was going to experience a lower low 20 years later that I discuss in an upcoming chapter of this book.

I felt horrible inside and out. After I treated my yeast infection, I put this sex episode behind me. It wasn't me. It never happened. It was too shameful and depraved, even for a sex addict like me.

And yet, a week or so later, I found myself driving 2-1/2 hours to see Joe from a dating website, because I got lost.

It was before GPS existed and I was determined to fuck.

Once I finally arrived at the desired destination, he told me I was 20 pounds heavier than my picture and that I had body odor. He was right on both. I was wearing polyester pants and my ass got sweaty from driving so long.

He was at least 20 years older than his photo and didn't smell so great either, so we were even.

12

Fucking for Survival

I'm on a blind, online date with this older flabby boring guy who has aspirations of being a professional musician. The men on these dates that I go on never look as good as their photo and never sound as suave.

I have been tortured by listening to samples of his music with his singing and guitar playing. I mean he sucked so badly. But, I was nice and told him he was pretty good and perhaps he will make it big one day.

We had a few drinks at a bar and we played pool. I hate playing pool with a guy I'm not into. When it was time to go home and we were in his car, he wanted to drive to a place a little more private before dropping me off. So he takes me to some remote, pitch-black, corner of a parking lot with warehouses or something like that, straight out of a Dateline episode.

He puts on a CD of his whiney music and starts making out with me and I'm like, ugh this guy is really gross, but I'm getting too scared to turn him down because what if he gets angry and starts to choke me out or something?

What is worse, fucking a nasty deadbeat musician or getting choked out dead and never seeing my family? No contest there. I fucked him to save my life.

13

The Fun Factor is Long Gone

Sex addiction is supposed to be fun, right? I mean why would I be addicted to something that wasn't fun or pleasurable?

I met Tom on Adult Friend Finder dot com and we had decent sex in a hotel.

In a subsequent communication, we discussed going on a sex date with his friend so we could have a threesome.

Oh wow, I was really excited and interested in that. I had never had a threesome and to do it with two guys was the stuff of my dreams!

We arranged to have dinner and then go to a hotel to fuck. Great!

The day of our date, sure enough, I got my period, heavy.

There was too much anticipation, planning, and commitment

up to this point that there was no way for me to cancel. But I was really upset that I was having my period and couldn't do sex the way I wanted to.

We had dinner and I drank a bottle or more of wine by myself, drowning my angst about my period in alcohol.

Mind you, I am a sex addict, but I am not a drinker.

On the car ride to the hotel, I had to ask Tom to pull over and I puked all over the sidewalk. Onward to the hotel.

We start kissing and making out and then it's time to pull down my pants and I'm all padded and tamponed up. I explain that we can still have sex but it may just be a little bit messier. Apparently, this was a total buzz kill.

I think the combination of me puking, still being drunk, and then having a bloody vagina was short of appealing for Tom and his friend.

They drove me home and that was the last I ever heard from them. This is definitely not fun.

The opposite of sex addiction is not abstinence. It is human connection, self-esteem, and peace of mind that everything will turn out okay.

14

Forever in Search of Extremes

L ike I previously mentioned, one website that I enjoyed was Adult Friend Finder. Fuck love and courting and going on magnificent dates, it was all about sex, and the kinkier the better.

That is how I found Master VanHof. He was the same age as my father at the time, 52 years. I was 27. He had man boobs. His dick did not work no matter how much I yanked and licked.

But, I hung in there so I could learn about and experience the BDSM lifestyle which sounded pretty intriguing to my escalating sexual tastes.

Master VanHof had a fascinating collection of artistic Japanese bondage books. He had a dungeon tool kit with all styles of whips, flogs, and feather dusters. It was very educational.

One evening, he hung me with ropes tied to my wrists to the ceiling pipes of his basement dungeon. He then proceeded to wrap me slowly, ankles up to my head with plastic cling wrap. He then made little holes for my nose and mouth so I could breathe.

I was anxiously waiting for the part where I would get turned on. Apparently, plastic wrap is not arousing for me. But alas, I tried.

Master VanHof entertained me with his spankings and rules. I had to tell him what I was wearing or eating when not with him. Of course I would lie about my food and never confess to a gallon of ice cream followed by a bag of chips. I had to wear a neck collar in his presence.

I have a tremendous attraction to dominant male personalities so I played along for a few months even though I was not attracted to him and the fact that he was my father's age definitely freaked me out.

Master VanHof took me on an island-getaway vacation. On the third day, he slapped me across the face because I didn't want to play along with his fetishes. I got on a plane and came home. I am fortunate that that is the only time I have been physically harmed by a man even though there were many circumstances when I could have ended up dead.

Thank you, Dear God for my life, Amen.

1. *Strong craving*
2. *Immediate gratification*
3. *Long-term consequences*
4. *Can't stop.*

15

Are There Any Good Looking Swingers?

Have you ever noticed that people at nude beaches are the last people that should be walking around nude? Likewise, it is with the swinger crowd.

When I used to fantasize about swinger parties, I imagined a Playboy Mansion party-type scene with all beautiful, happy people, dancing and swaying, and loving on each other.

Likely there are beautiful, vibrant swinger people out there, but they tend to be unicorns. I went to a swinger party once. Once was enough.

Alcohol was forbidden so that everything conformed to consensuality rules. Okay, no problem, but two glasses of wine would have helped.

This is where the dichotomy comes in. On the one hand, I want to have every orifice filled with a throbbing cock and explode in waves of orgasm. On the other hand, I am a "good girl" and I don't belong here. Plus, these people are the most unattractive, messed up people, who need to take stock of their own issues. Now mind you, with my other torrid affair with disordered eating, I am very accepting of bigger bodies and people's health journeys. But if you want to get off on your sex addiction fantasies, all that shit goes out the window. I want beautiful people to fuck damn it!

There was a lady with spina bifida who was at the swinger party with her able-bodied boyfriend. They didn't swap with anyone, but they took advantage of a suspended swing so they could have sex easier. I was so happy for them. Since I have a fondness for any person with a disability, especially one who is ambulatory with a wheelchair, that was really the highlight of the evening for me. I hope they have a wonderful life together.

As for me, I needed to get off on something to complete my evening. There was a Sybian vibration machine that I sat on, while blindfolded, and spectators watched. Yes, dirty, kinky, novel, thrilling...for 3 minutes. Then back to reality.

It's 3 am. I need to drive home 1-1/2 hours away. I'm so tired. I'm lonely. Why did I do that? It was a waste of time. I should be home in bed and sleeping. I'm going to be tired tomorrow and compromised for my long day at work and the kids.

1. *Strong craving*
2. *Immediate gratification*
3. *Long-term consequences*
4. *Can't stop.*

16

Toxic Triangles

I n my sex addiction days, love triangles were fair game. I would shoot a Sex Eye at husbands and boyfriends. The gaze was often reciprocated.

It usually didn't materialize into any physical contact, but it was just enough vibe for any female friends to feel the tension and discourage any deeper friendship. It was clear that I was not to be trusted and that I was a homewrecker.

To me, it was just another momentary thrill to be naughty and secretive. And a sick validation of my feminine charms and physical attractiveness.

I was at my friend's party, and her hot-looking fiancee offered to walk me to my car because it was late and dark. Sure enough, he gave me (or was it I who gave him?) a nice, passionate, sexy kiss before I got in my car. Taboo, wrong, sinful. I loved it! And I hated myself. That was the last I ever saw of this friend.

It was like this with my high school best friend and her love interests, friends from college, friends as an adult.

I would always make it a contest about whether I could woo the guy with my feminine wiles.

I didn't act on it most of the time, but it was naughty and nice to know that I could have it if I wanted to. It was my little secret just between me and the guy.

I was fucked up and that's why I always thought that if someone truly knew me, they would hate me.

17

Food/Fuck Flip Flop

According to addiction experts, 98% of addicts have more than one type of addiction. It is common to have concurrent sex addiction with alcohol dependence or drug abuse. For me, my co-addiction was disordered eating and binge eating.

At 35 years old, I was already in a serious relationship for 7 years with my now husband, Richard. Since I was sexing less and eating more, I had put on quite a bit of weight. I needed a fast and effective way to lose this weight since my efforts at dieting were making me fatter.

I went to The Phenomenal Hypnotist, William. William was very expensive because he was so amazing at his profession. He charged me a solid mortgage payment for his services, so it had to be good, right?

He worked from his basement. His house smelled like ferrets, as in the animal.

I am a die-hard animal lover, but nobody's house should smell like a ferret.

I started my hypnosis session while standing upright, and focused on a pendulum swinging back and forth. He was saying some hypnosis mumbo jumbo in his soft hypnotic voice, proceeded by counting. Then, I laid down on his ferrety couch and allowed my now hypnotized mind to be told to stop eating like a pig and that ice cream will taste like shit on a spoon to me.

I didn't realize it at the moment, but this "lying still" thing with a man sitting over me talking tender bullshit was actually turning me on.

Over the next few days, I hardly ate. I was giddy and floating around like a moth.

I had to text William to tell him how miraculous his hypnosis was and that it was definitely working because I ate like a "normal person," or possibly even less. He was very pleased and said that our next session will build on this success. He was right!

For our second session, I was feeling better about myself, and I wore my cute red wrap skirt and a low-cut blouse with my boobs peeking out. We started with the pendulum bullshit accompanied by counting, and me laying down on the smelly, ferrety couch.

I lay with my eyes closed as he jibber-jabbered over me. Even though my eyes were closed, I could easily feel how close his face was to mine and I could feel the movement of his eyes across my body. That felt really, really goooood. Now I realized that I was enjoying hypnosis a little bit too much.

The next few days, even less of an appetite! I was just high on life. I recall dancing around and singing to the song "*Serenade from the Stars*" by Steve Miller Band, while making breakfast which was much smaller than my usual.

I kept thinking back to my hypnosis sessions and how enjoyable and relaxing they were and how I loved the sound of William's voice.

The pounds were already coming off. I needed to keep texting William about my progress and his amazing talents.

I went back for a third session. Pendulum, counting, jibber jabber...tongue. It was on. We were on.

William had a wife and three kids and I was in a serious relationship and had three kids. It was good because we both had to be discreet. As I got to know William, I liked him less and less.

He was ugly inside and out. He would crush up Percocet pills and sniff them. He lived like a pig and he had poor hygiene. He was a porn addict. He had bad financial debts and he had bad business reviews accusing him of stealing people's money.

I looked right past all this and saw him as an opportunity to get my sexual thrills. We saw each other very rarely and it was always a disappointment when we did see each other. Most of our relationship was via email and sexting.

I had fantasies of Richard and me being friends with William and his wife and that we would hang out together and swap spouses, eat dinners together, and hang out on the couch as friends.

On one occasion, William and I met in a supermarket parking lot. I was craving attention and tenderness. I ended up just having my face pushed down onto his smelly dick because he was in a hurry and needed to get back home to his wife. He took photos of me the whole time.

One day William said that another of his hot female clients fell in lust with him and wanted to have sex with him. Her name was Amelia and she was very sexually free and was open to having a threesome with us.

The planning for this threesome, where, when, how, and what took many weeks. I was absolutely obsessed with the anticipation of this very hot get-together.

However, Richard was on to me.

It's hard to be consistently secretive.

He would notice me texting constantly and clinging to my cell phone and getting on the computer constantly. He noticed me rapidly losing weight and acting sassier.

I was down 25 pounds over the course of these 6 months.

The night before I was supposed to meet William and Amelia at a hotel, Richard had a massive, explosive, emotional breakdown. Apparently, he had been spying on me for some time and knew all the details. I was always leaving my computer open to my emails and websites so it wasn't that challenging actually. I thought he trusted me and wouldn't look, but he did. And he was right.

That threesome never happened.

Richard broke up with me.

I cried. I begged. I pleaded. I stalked him and left food and flowers on his car hood at work. I wrote letters, emails, and cards. I did everything I could to get him back.

Since I was living with my children and parents, my mom witnessed my devastation and knew the reason. I was really embarrassed.

I was horrified at what I had done. I couldn't stand William. He was absolutely repulsive to me, yet I stayed in a fucked up sex relationship with him for 6 whole months.

On the other hand, I absolutely loved and appreciated Richard throughout the entire duration of our relationship. I had no intention of ever leaving Richard or even feeling unhappy in the slightest way.

It took a few weeks for Richard to even talk to me. When he eventually came back to me he asked if I was a sex addict. I was like, "What?! What's that?"

I looked up what the term meant, and yes! Yes, indeed I was a sex addict! My problem had a name. "Yes, I admit that I am a sex addict."

Richard advised that I go to therapy, so I did. It was helpful at the time. I gained a lot of insight. It helped heal our relationship. It helped Richard to understand my behavior more and to have reinforcement that there wasn't anything wrong in what he was doing as a partner.

However, this betrayal did create long lasting damage to his trust in me. And it made our beautiful relationship less innocent.

Years later, when I was able to regain more of his trust, I would break his heart again. And again. Each time making it more and more difficult to recover.

The therapist pointed out the inverse relationship between overeating and oversexing behaviors which were not noticed until this point.

I promised Richard that I would never cheat on him again. I gained back the 25 pounds in 6 weeks or less.

Admitting that I have a sex addiction was the first step in disarming it, but I needed a lot more work over the next 15 years.

18

Binge Eating is my Other Drug

My earliest memory of binge eating was at age 12 years, when my sexual abuse ended. At that time I had a babysitting job which made it easy to eat all the candy and hide the evidence.

I did not learn how to eat until this past year. And I'm still working on it. It sounds odd to not know how to eat, but this is what I mean...

Food was a substance for my comfort, pleasure, and abuse. If something tasted good, I wanted more. I could not stop eating it until it was all gone. This was the case with cookies, ice cream, chips, cake, cheese, bread, whatever.

If I had to eat with friends and family at a social gathering, I would need to concentrate and focus on not eating like the pig that I wanted to be. Even with white knuckling around food, I still either overate to the point of feeling ill or I barely ate so that I could stay in control, often times the discomfort of being with other people made me eat less.

In private, I would devour the house. Often I would try to be "healthy," focusing on more protein and whole foods, but it would only last so long.

To compensate, I was on every type of diet pill and diet plan.

I severely restricted my food to compensate for overeating and then I would binge harder when the hunger kicked in.

I would go through packages of cookies, bags of chips, cartons of ice cream, packages of cheese, all of this and more, in one sitting...I would feel so sick to my stomach, bloated, exhausted, nauseous, with abdominal pain and shit storms. I just wanted to lay there and pass out like a heroin junkie, but I needed to go to work, take care of the kids, do my responsibilities. Although it felt like self-torture every single time, I did it anyway.

I would consume 3 days worth of food in one sitting, and therefore in my mind I would try to use the next 3 days of not eating to recover.

Moderation was not in my vocabulary in most aspects of my life.

I went to Overeaters Anonymous meetings for close to one year but the 12-Step Approach did not fully resonate with me. I liked the motto, "Take what you need, and leave the rest", as it pertained to the information provided. I loved the first step of surrendering my addiction to my Higher Power. I was truly powerless over food. But from there, there was never a resolution to regain your power over food. At OA, they practice food abstinence which means that similar to an alcoholic, a food addict can never eat a sugary or fatty food in moderation. The cookie always wins. To me, OA was just another diet.

At a height of 5'3", my highest weight was 185 lb and my lowest was 123 lb. I would lose and gain 30 pounds from one year to the next for decades, mostly varying from 135 to 165 pounds.

It didn't look that significant to acquaintances that I came across. Only I knew the extent of the damage, body criticism, and physical abuse that I put myself through.

19

It Was Hard To Be Married to Me

Richard and I met online in the infancy of internet dating in 2000. We had a spicey start to our relationship since we were both coming out of divorce and sowing our oats all over the place.

While we were on/off and casual for a while, it evolved into a serious relationship over the course of two years.

Richard was the only man that I bothered to sleep in bed with until the morning after we had sex. I would go to his apartment after the kids were asleep and stay the night.

In the morning, Richard would brew coffee, then put the coffee cup on a saucer and give me a teaspoon. That detail of the coffee presentation was a loving gesture and something I attribute to me bonding with Richard and eventually falling in love with him.

He knew I wanted to eat ice cream for breakfast, not eggs,

and always made sure to have some in his freezer. I would drink coffee and eat all the ice cream in his freezer and it was just pure sex/food ecstasy when I was with Richard. Likewise, Richard thought it was amusing that I would be naked in his kitchen, drinking coffee, and pigging out on ice cream.

Richard was handsome and kind and gentle and loving and artistic. He was also a father. When I officially got involved in a relationship with Richard, his wonderful daughter, age 11, was included in my commitment to him.

He loved me through the span of a 50-pound yo-yo in my weight. He told me that he loved me and that I looked beautiful at any size.

He took me in as a whole package with my three little kids. He was loving and accepting and helpful with my disabled son, Alex.

But, it was hard to have me as a wife or girlfriend. I was a bit bored with vanilla and consistently looking for ways to spice up the relationship that pushed boundaries a bit too far. Richard would ask, "Why can't you just calm down and be content and happy with "regular sex?"

I was always chasing some sort of thrill.

Sex toys, extra huge dildos, lingerie, porn– that's all fair game in a loving relationship and we did all that. But I wanted more.

I wanted to go to nude beaches, tantric sex workshops, swinger clubs, and sex resorts. I wanted to solicit a woman (he wouldn't even entertain the thought of a man) to join us for sex. And Richard obliged me on all of these things. He went way out of his comfort zone to go to Hedonism Resort in Jamaica, which is a swinger's resort. He went to nude beaches, and tantric sex workshops, and searched online for women to join us for threesomes.

I would accuse Richard of being "boring" sexually. It was very hard on him and all the while, he was never the problem. I always loved my husband and found him super attractive and felt very gratified with our sex and intimacy. It was just my sex addiction talking. I often dressed provocatively and when I drove in the car I would intentionally hike up my skirt so male drivers in higher cars could see me as they passed in the lane next to me. Perhaps it may sound appealing to have a wife like this, but in reality it diminishes the strength of the relationship. It chips away at a man's security, leaving him to feel emasculated and inadequate.

If you are not okay with your wife having sex with another man, you would probably also be concerned that she must not be satisfied.

It would make you feel like something was wrong with you if your wife wanted sex outside of the relationship. You would never want your wife to make you feel like that.

Of course, whenever Richard would catch me acting on my sex addiction, I would beg and plead and explain that it was not about him at all.

I was always happy with Richard and he was always The One. But, to a person who doesn't have a sex addiction, it's really hard to understand.

In Maté's book, In the Realm of Hungry Ghosts, in the chapter regarding behavioral addictions, he states that a relationship with a sex addict just won't last. The quest for novel experiences is such that no relationship can withstand.

It seems that Richard and I are the exception.

I see Richard as my angel from heaven since I adamantly believe in Divine Intervention. Richard has kept me safe from seeking more outside relationships than I already have. In the psychology world, perhaps Richard would be called the co-dependent partner.

I don't see it that way. Richard was the kid that would try to save a bird that fell out of the nest, or a baby squirrel that was orphaned. He is a "saver" and a helper and a fixer. Perhaps I was just another squirrel for him to save, but I believe we are indeed soul mates.

He displays his love with his actions, by doing things that are difficult or involve sacrifice. He takes care of his elderly mother, our kids, and me. For that I am eternally grateful.

Richard was also really skilled at recognizing my sex addiction behavior even when I couldn't. He would say that I wear my emotions on my sleeve and that ultimately I am very bad at being secretive and stealthy. When I was misbehaving, he knew. He would call it out as my addiction, trying to bring me into sobriety.

As it turns out, Richard was very successful at limiting my opportunities, decreasing my risk tolerance, and decreasing my interest in acting out. It was because he provided me with love, security, and stability. However, my addiction was such that I would still occasionally act out despite Richard's unwavering love, if the opportunity arose. Richard's intentions were innocent when he gave me massage gift certificates for my birthday.

On one occasion I got a happy ending. I decided to tell him that I did that because I ultimately felt guilty that somehow he was "enabling" me by giving me such a gift, even though I knew that he would never want to do such a thing.

Of course, he no longer bought massage gift certificates for me. And, the truth is, I was relieved that he was adamant about not enabling me to act out.

Thank you, dear Richard, for not giving up on our relationship when there were so many reasons to. Till death do us part.

Do any of your behaviors make the people in your life believe it is their fault that you behave this way?

20

"Working" For Free

I had sex with 6 guys at the same time for free. I had sex with old, ugly, fat dudes for free. I sucked a guy's cock on a bathroom floor for free. I didn't like the sex and I didn't even get paid! Sex workers get paid.

They also would likely not do their job if they had financial independence. And here I was, doing these dirty deeds, for free.

I thought if I'm doing it for free and part of the reason I am doing extreme sexual behaviors is to escape the stress of financial insecurity, then I should just become a paid sex worker.

It was annoying to be a pediatrician because I was certainly far from being a "rich doctor." Pediatricians were the lowest-paid type of doctor and I was just starting my career and supporting three kids and paying Alex's medical bills and for nannies, and life was just expensive.

I looked into how I could become a call girl, but it was too difficult to become established in that and still be a full-time mom, and pediatrician, and have a serious boyfriend who would not be on board with that.

Plus, I lived in my parent's house for the first 10 years of my kids' life and it would just be too difficult to be a professional prostitute. But, I contemplated it very seriously. Of course I romanticized it thinking it would be just like the movie "Pretty Woman" and I would have someone handsome like Richard Gere showering me with gifts and affection. Clearly, it was my sex addiction talking and it was only the difficult logistics that kept me from doing it.

But then, I got another brilliant idea instead. I used to be a big fan of The Howard Stern Show.

There was a radio personality, from The Stern Show, who was a fucked up cocaine-addicted comedian that I absolutely adored. He was crazy-funny, vulnerable, and real.

He often talked about how he would pay $20,000 to have sex with a hot girl because, he joked, no hot girl would have sex with him for free.

Hell, I would do it for $5K.

I got on a bus to New York City and I showed up at the location of the radio show so I could meet this radio personality and offer myself. Perhaps I wasn't "hot" enough, but that's not the point. I was desperate for money and having sex with the radio personality would not have been bad at all because I was genuinely a fan. Fortunately or unfortunately, I was stopped by the security guards and unable to make my offer.

I thought if people could read my mind about my wishes to be a sex worker when I was already working as a pediatrician and mom to little children, everybody would think I was a sick person and never be my friend or ever want anything to do with me.

Repeatedly, I thought that if someone truly knew me, they would hate me.

This pervasive thought made it impossible for me to make any meaningful friendships, or have any meaningful human connections outside of my children and Richard.

I just felt like the most fucked up person in the world.

What would people's opinion of you be if they knew about your extreme sexual tastes and behaviors?

What if you didn't give a fuck what their opinion of you was? What if it only matters what your opinion is of yourself?

21

Prioritizing My Own Self-Destruction

I had my own medical private practice for 10 years. My morning routine would be to get up early to get my kids ready for school.

Alex was disabled so he always needed full assistance to get out of bed and into his wheelchair, brush his teeth, groom, get dressed, and puke.

He was a puker and puked every morning before school due to all his medical issues. I would make sure everyone's bags and snacks and lunch money are prepared, load up the car, and drop them at school.

Then I would go to a coffee shop and buy a couple of donuts and a sugar slushie drink. I would drive to my office and then enjoy up to one hour of relaxation after my morning rush.

My relaxation consisted of eating and drinking my sugar and fat-laden breakfast while watching free internet porn. Locked away in my office, with no one to disturb me until my office hours started. I would be worked up into an ecstatic, aroused state by 10 am. My favorite porn category was MMF which means two men on one woman and also massage leading to sex.

If someone wanted to come in earlier than 10 am, I was thrown off my game. I mean, life is hard, and I needed my porn and donut time to start my day off on the right foot.

Porn and donuts were very important to me and I made sure to make time in my schedule for this every single fucking day, for years. The busier and crazier my life got, the more I would prioritize my sex time.

Even if I worked 10-hour days and ran around to physical therapy with Alex, and sports and school events with my three kids, I still would make time to go out on an internet date escapade after the kids were asleep.

Of course, this made me tired and cranky for my daytime responsibilities. But such is the evil of addiction- it steals joy from your life and then convinces you that you need more of the addiction to experience that joy.

Addiction made me think that I was successfully juggling motherhood, working full-time, AND a sex addiction! I am quite the over-achiever. There must be some sort of trophy for such a feat!

Now that I have no interest in porn and do not engage in sex addiction behaviors, I also lost my taste for donuts.

Do you ever make time and prioritize your addiction to the detriment of time with your family or job responsibilities?

Are you more tired than you should be because you spend time on your sex addiction rather than getting sleep and rest?

1. Strong craving
2. Short-term gratification
3. Long-term consequences.
4. Can't stop.

22

Internet Makes Access Easy

I don't know how people engaged in sex addiction prior to the invention of online dating. I know there were "seeking" ads in the back of newspapers but still, it's just not the same level of easy access.

It is also very likely that sex and food addiction didn't even exist thousands of years ago or a few hundred, or even a hundred years ago because people were busy using all of their resources to survive.

Sex and food were primal instincts for survival.

Sure, they were pleasurable, but perhaps there was not enough opportunity to overdose on them repeatedly so that it would be considered an addiction.

Now, sex and food addiction is enabled by the abundance and easy access to it in our society.

"Hello, Beautiful. You're so sexy. Your lips are so hot." I ate up all this stuff. I totally got off on these perceived compliments. I loved seeing a long, long list of responses from random, mostly anonymous online dudes vying for my attention.

Ashley Madison was an online dating site that catered specifically to people that are already in committed relationships and are looking for a discreet affair. This was just perfect for a sex addict like me.

I could keep my relationship with Richard, and fuck around on the side. Perfect!

I never actually went through with meeting men in person at that time because Richard could immediately "read" my behavior when I would try to arrange a date. I only went as far as explicit emails and making plans that didn't materialize.

It felt like Richard was always watching me but in retrospect, he was keeping me safe from myself.

23

My Mind Makes My Body Sick

J ust short of my 40th birthday I was diagnosed with non-Hodgkin's Lymphoma. "What the hell Godddd! Fuck you! Don't we already have enough problems?! You need to teach me more lessons?! Like, oh I have to appreciate life more...not take things for granted...well FUCK YOU God! I don't need your god-damn fuckin' lessons!" I thought that God gave me cancer. Really, it was I that gave myself cancer.

My world was shattered.

I was a mom of 3 teenage children, one of whom was disabled. I was a working mom, supporting my family with my small medical practice.

Now all my fears were coming true.
My health was threatened.
My safety and financial security were threatened.
My life was threatened!
My kids had to suffer having a mother with cancer and all the

fears associated with this.

It was quite a shock.

I underwent difficult chemo for 5 months. While undergoing chemo, Alex underwent a horrifying scoliosis repair surgery with spinal fusion from his neck to his sacrum. He was in the hospital for two months due to complications and his recovery took an additional year for him to be somewhat functional.

When I was feeling weak and exhausted from chemo, sitting in the hospital with Alex while he had excruciating pain and mysterious post-operative fevers that were medical anomalies. I felt total, utter, bottomless despair. Despite my anger at God/The Universe, I still called out for help to my Higher Power. In these moments of complete defeat and hopelessness, even a Godless person such as myself, could only beg for help from something that was greater than human. "Please God, help us. We need your help."

I was depressed and did a lot of unhealthy comfort eating. I experienced resentment at God and the Universe to allow this health crisis to happen when life was already difficult enough. I became increasingly angry at my first husband for not helping enough with the children during my illness. I also had to close my medical practice. I was financially, physically, and emotionally crushed. My sadness, anger, and resentments raged on.

Time passed and we got through it.

I really don't like the term "cancer survivor" or " I beat cancer." I survived by the grace of God. He allowed me to live and for Alex to recover.

I had the support of my husband, Richard, and my close family.

It was certainly not because my will was stronger than cancer or that I did anything extraordinary about my illness. I just did my chemo and hoped for the best.

My cancer had presented with a large chicken egg size tumor in my left inguinal lymph nodes, close to my genital area.

Louise Hay, author of *You Can Heal Your Life*, the guru of mind-body health and healing, had suffered from a cancerous tumor near her vaginal area.

She had written in her books that after enduring sexual abuse as a child and having dysfunctional thoughts about her genitalia, it was no surprise that a cancerous tumor would grow in that body part.

She worked for years on healing her mind and body and shared her insights through several amazing self-help books.

Likewise, it was no surprise that my cancer would be in my inguinal area, very close to my genitals. That was a source of disease in my mind and it manifested as a cancerous tumor in my body. One would think I would heed these alarm bells...nope, I did not.

As part of my recovery after chemotherapy, I took classes at the School of Burlesque. I saw it as an opportunity to get my sexy back. I could dance around to music and wear sparkly costumes, and get naked all for the sake of performance art.

At age 42 years, I became Paulina PanTease, burlesque performer extraordinaire. My burlesque stage name inspired the pseudonym for this book, Paulina Pantyleva.

I enjoyed my budding career as a burlesque dancer. Paulina was my alter-ego, full of confidence, joy, and celebration. Burlesque was a fun hobby for a year.

I met many burlesque performers who I prejudged to be confident, carefree and creative people. In actuality, I found that most, if not all, burlesque performers were also suffering personal torment of some sort that made them gravitate towards burlesque art as their therapy.

Richard is a talented photographer and we made some beautiful boudoir photos during this time. I even had a monthly burlesque show in my little suburb.

"Tastefully stripping" in a sparkly costume was just another acting out of my sex addiction. Albeit not as risky or sordid as fucking some nasty dude in the back seat of a car so I wouldn't get slashed.

I did some major sexting and had numerous sexual conversations with men online as Paulina PanTease during this time. That was a break from my promise to Richard after the Hypnotist William ordeal. I just wanted to hear the usual, "You're so beautiful. You're so hot. I want you so bad." Blah, blah, blah. It all sounds so boring, empty, and stupid now as I write about this.

Do you try to act out your sex addiction in less risky ways while still feeding your addiction?

24

I Broke

The story of Danny Tango.

This is the most painful story for me to write about because it is the most recent and it was the final straw for me to fix my fucked up mind and stop this fucked up cycle. This sexual episode was also different from past experiences because rather than remaining entirely secretive, I became so infatuated, in a record speed short time of three weeks, that I actually wanted to leave Richard for another man.

At age 48, I wrecked my family. My vase which represented the wholeness and security of my family life was shattered. I was completely broken and lifeless, because if you take away my husband and destroy my family, make my children and parents cry, you have essentially killed me.

I begged and cried for weeks for Richard to take me back. I apologized to each member of my family that I had hurt and made them cry. Despite my apologies and contrition, I definitely caused permanent damage and trauma to my family.

They could never look at me the same again.

I have the date of my break up with Richard noted on my google calendar to repeat every year so I never ever forget what I did.

It's not meant as a forever punishment, but I want to always remember where I came from now that years are passing and I am cured of my sex addiction.

I want to always remember the hard-earned learning lessons and continue growing in wisdom so that I can help myself and others.

I had been solidly faithful to Richard for the past 7 years. My disordered eating raged with weight gain and loss every year of 20 to 30 pounds. I was in a phase of my lowest weight in a very long time.

I was exercising regularly and feeling better about my body but still wanted to get smaller. People were asking me if I was okay which was a tremendous compliment to a fucked up body dysmorphic person like me.

At the onset of this incident, I remember having some minor sexual fantasy stuff swirling around in my head, but nothing too major.

I decided to attend a new dance studio for an Argentine Tango class. Tango Danny was the teacher and it felt like fireworks when I saw him and we locked eyes. It's very impressive how our endorphins can release like that and create a high.

It was a group lesson, but I got all the attention from him. The Spell was cast. I couldn't stop thinking about the lesson and how wonderful I felt in our tango embrace. Now, in retrospect, it's a horrible sickening memory.

The next day the texting starts. "The lesson was great and I want to come in for private lessons." The conversation quickly turned into mind crack. Danny was a Master. He was dominant and kinky and said things that blew my fucking mind to the moon and back again. He was a professional dancer and since I love dancing and admire professional dancers, these attributes catapulted my fantasies into overdrive. This is where Sex Addiction lives after all, in the Mind.

It is Addiction to Fantasy. I quickly became obsessed and infatuated with having a Tango Master as a lover. Danny told me that he wanted to groom and take care of me like Christine from Phantom of the Opera.

He made me watch the movie The Secretary (2002 with Maggie Gyllenhaal and James Spader).
He sent me tango music playlists I had to listen to.
He sent me artwork.
He spoke to me in five different languages.
I would lay in bed and fantasize about him and listen to his music and masturbate.

After only a week's time, I had been brainwashed into thinking that Danny and I were going to run off together...I would learn the tango and we would be dance partners performing all over the world.

Our spectacular love and dynamic would magically fix all the "loose ends" in our life, like him having to live with his young daughter, him having little income, and me having a husband, and content life in the status quo.

We went out to lunch the second week of our initial meeting. His car was a hoarder's paradise. He certainly didn't have the outward look of Mr. Grey.

After eating we went for a walk and returned to our cars. That is where the KISS happened. It happened in the parking garage of the mall.

You know those scary movies about demons or aliens and they lock onto a person's mouth and nose and suck the soul out of them? And it looks like this steamy smokey dark particle type stuff that comes out, leaving the suck-ee all weak and lifeless as the suck-er gets all strong and powerful?

That was us. I lost my soul that day.

In the next week, I was even more possessed by my own fantasies. I had completely lost my mind. I was not in this world. I needed to break up with Richard so that I could go to Danny.

I didn't want to cheat on Richard as I did in the past so I wanted to tell him that I met a man whom I was infatuated with. And even though it has been only three weeks since I have known him, I needed to follow my heart and soul to the world of Danny.

Richard says, "Let me understand...You met a guy 3 weeks ago and you want to break up with me? Do you want to throw away over 20 years of our relationship? After everything I have done for you, raising our kids, helping you with Alex, helping you with your businesses, helping you with your house, you want to break up with me?"
I reply, "Yes."
Richard responds, "Is this your sex addiction talking? You have lost a lot of weight recently."
To which I deny, "No, no. This is real."

Richard hung in there for four more days trying to change my mind and fight for me, and then he was gone.

My mom was crying. My daughter was crying. My two sons were crying. The dogs were crying. The cat was crying. I was crying. The fish were crying. The fly on the wall was crying. This is what I had done.

I was now alone and I told Danny that I had broken up with my husband for him and that we were good to go to have our dreamy life together.
Danny said, "Really?! Why would you do that?"

That same day, Danny asked me for money and miraculously the spell was broken. Just like that.

"Hello, Richard. I made a terrible mistake. Please come home...."

25

My Rock Bottom

I t is said that once the pain of the addiction is greater than the reward, that is when change occurs. The gap between the Danny Tango Spell breaking and Richard coming home to me was my bottoming out.

The pain was unbearable.

I lay in my bed realizing what I had done. My sobriety sank in, drowning me in memories and thoughts of the past twenty years.

I had thrown away a precious twenty year relationship. Richard was the one that had stayed with me through all of life's trials, parenting struggles, health crisis's, financial struggles, fun vacations, travel adventures, prior betrayals and forgiveness, family milestones, business struggles, our hopes, dreams, and all the colors of life.

Love is an action. Richard had demonstrated love for me for the duration of our relationship.

I prayed and pleaded for Richard to return to me.

I apologized to my children and parents.

I allowed myself to fully feel the pain so that I remembered forever to never ever create such devastation again.

Of course, I had made similar promises to myself in the past, but this pain was the deepest yet. I knew I had to find definitive help, somehow. I just didn't know how at that moment.

III

My Recovery

26

The Healing is Spiritual

Richard had come back to me, but after the Danny Tango fiasco, I was weak. I was tired. I couldn't self-regulate my eating or sleeping or emotions. I was walking around like a zombie, soul-less, and drained.

Three weeks into this, I was doing an errand, picking up a skirt from a local tailor shop. I had been a customer there for several years, but didn't know the two owners, Jerry and Juan, on any significant level.

I walked in and sat on a bench while they were helping some other customers.

When it was my turn, Juan says, " What's the matter? You don't look like yourself." I explained that I was just feeling very run down and tired and sad.

"Why sad?" he asks.

"Because I met a person that I trusted who turned out to be very bad and there's just stress in my life and I don't feel like myself."

Jerry, overhearing this, starts explaining that there are people in this world that are evil and suck energy. They cast spells on people with their charms whether it be good looks, talent, or intelligence. These good graces provide a front against their true evil nature. To get your energy and soul back when encountering such a person, one must simply say to yourself, "God is with Me."

"God is with you, Paulina. There, now you have your soul back."

I couldn't believe what he was telling me. It's like he read my energy, my look, my thoughts. I instantly felt better. While it still took me a year to figure stuff out, the day I got my soul back was a crucial start.

I am not particularly religious, but I am spiritual.

Suddenly, it made me look back on small and big events in my life that seemed random, and now it felt more magnetic or destined. When I was a teenager traveling in Europe, somehow I would be the one who would have a man jerking off under a newspaper in my train car. I would be the one with a peeping Tom in my dorm. I would be the one discreetly dry-humped by a passenger on a swaying bus.

It felt like the Universe conspired to put me in hyper-sexualized situations. However, the Universe/God also brought me into the tailor shop that day, to explain to me how to get my soul back.

And God made it possible for me to meet my Mindset Coach, Dana, a few months later because nothing, absolutely nothing happens by chance. God is with me.

I take full responsibility for everything that has happened to me, good or bad, and that mindset empowers me to not be a victim of circumstance. No matter how seemingly random an event is, I attracted it. I am now coming to the profound understanding as to why these things have happened over the course of my life. It turns out, they had a purpose.

Do you feel like you have more than your fair share of problems, struggles, and unfortunate events?

Perhaps there is actually an order, reason, purpose, and greater good for these things even if you don't know why?

What if you subconsciously attracted these things thinking you needed to be punished for something?

What if you can ultimately control such things?

What if "everything is the way it's supposed to be", wouldn't it be a more peaceful way to live?

What if everything that has happened is actually your superpower, your wisdom, and your gift to the world? ***Even if it was sucking a lot of cock.***

27

The Problem Had Been in My Mind

Mothers are really good at feeling guilty. I felt guilty for my secretive and naughty sexual escapades of course. I felt guilty that I was cheating on my husband and family.

However, the guilt that ate me up more than anything was the thought that I caused my son, Alex's, disability.

I was in my fourth year of medical school and I wanted to get pregnant asap, so that I could graduate, have a baby, and start my residency.

I was a Type A personality, and all of my life goals had to be done on my terms, on my timeline, no matter how much I had to manipulate something to achieve my goals in a timely manner. Since I had a delay of several months in getting pregnant, I requested a fertility drug to help me get pregnant right away. Since I was a medical student, I had easier access to informal medical requests for unnecessary medications (work culture has changed since then of course).

Before my kids were born, I used to be horrified at the sight of a disabled person. I would divert my eyes and try my best to avoid interacting with anyone who had a disability. Because of this, I felt the Universe wanted to punish me by giving me a disabled child so that I could learn my life's lessons.

I felt angry and resentful that my innocent, beautiful child, Alex, would be allowed to suffer the consequences of his severe disability so that I could learn my lessons. I became pregnant with triplets (by taking a pill I didn't need), and I did not do my proper bed rest and delivered early, and it was ALL my fault.

I was angry that Alex was born disabled so I could learn a lesson. My anger, guilt, and shame would manifest in various situations throughout the next twenty years.

What does behavior that causes guilt deserve? It deserves to be punished.

More so, this is a subconscious feeling and one that I wasn't fully aware of.

The feeling of guilt can be like a magnet- bad things occur more often, seemingly randomly and for the purposes of punishment. I began to feel like a dark cloud was following me and that somehow I was not meant to succeed. I experienced depression and tried the typical anti-depressant medications. The medications didn't work. They can't replace mindset work.

The only medication that "worked" was getting lost in porn, seeking random sexual encounters, binging on cookies, cake, and ice cream, and fantasizing about sex.

When I found my Mindset Coach, Dana, she helped me to fully accept Alex's disability and helped me disarm my guilt.

I now see Alex's disability and the fact that I am his mother as our soul's journey. Alex's soul and my soul chose each other.

Nothing I did could have caused or prevented Alex's disability. The universe meant for us to be together in this situation, to play out whatever we needed to learn.

Alex has been here before. It was not his first time meeting me on this earth.

According to mind-body expert Louise Hay, cerebral palsy's spiritual meaning is "to bring the family together" While there was much additional stress and difficult sibling dynamics, the family and I, somehow, are better for it.

I feel better knowing there is a purpose, even if I don't know all the answers to the "whys".

Even if Dana and I are wrong about this soul journey thing, it is a more peaceful way to live to believe in this. I choose to have peace of mind due to my beliefs.

I am more joyful and experience life more calmly and with contentment. I choose happiness.

If you need help seeing your past traumas in a way where that enhances you rather than traumatizes you, find a trusted mindset coach or therapist.

Healing can happen only when you make sense of the traumas of the past.

The feeling of guilt caused me to feel shame, seek punishment, seek escape from my negative emotions, and as a result, stole all the joy out of my life. Ultimately, it was a wasted emotion, because feeling guilty solved absolutely nothing.

Do you have a family member in your life that causes you tremendous stress, hardship, or possibly guilt? Consider thinking about it as " There is nothing that could have prevented this situation because the Universe/God meant for it to be this way. We are soul mates and meant to be together for better or worse. There are gifts in this circumstance, should I choose to find them." Throw your guilt or shame to the wind.

It does not serve you and only steals your joy. It causes you to act on your addictions to self-medicate.

What if you chose to be happy despite the stress, pressure, and emotional pain? A person can have pain and stay happy.

28

Making Sense of the Nonsense

"**T**his is the domain of addiction, where we constantly seek something outside ourselves to curb an insatiable yearning for relief or fulfillment. The aching emptiness is perpetual because the...pursuits we hope will soothe it are not what we really need."
~ Gabor Maté MD

I was completely unaware of my own emotional signals. I thought that I was hungry for ice cream or donuts or cake, but I was really hungry for rest, comfort, safety, and security.

My mind and body would confound loneliness, and sadness, and overwhelm with a need to fuck a stranger or engorge myself with junk food. In retrospect it seems so clear what I was truly hungry for yet, at the moment, my hunger was mutated into a misinterpreted signal.

I binge ate donuts, sweet coffee slushies, ice cream, and comfort foods. I starved myself to compensate. I binge-exercised to make up for overeating. I was hyper-focused on my body and always trying to lose weight. I equated a lower weight with happiness and success.

As a result of working with Coach Dana, I learned the following: The opposite of disordered eating is not eating in moderation. The opposite of disordered eating is eating, exercising, talking, thinking, and acting as if you love yourself. The opposite of disordered eating is self-love, acceptance, and living in authenticity.

If the goal is eating in moderation, it's really just another diet by a different name. Moderation is the side effect of healing your relationship with your shadows, traumas, and resentments. Moderation is the side effect of healing my relationship with food. It is the result of working through the real underlying causes of my dysfunction.

Now I am able to eat socially. I destroy myself with food, far less often. I enjoy exercise in moderation. I enjoy junk foods in moderation. I am more selective with the quality and quantity of my food.Is it perfect? Far from it, but it's better.

What were some childhood and teen behaviors and attitudes surrounding food, family, love, and health beliefs that formed your adult eating behaviors?

Do you have certain beliefs about foods that create food rules for yourself?

What if the rules are- there are no rules?

29

Embracing My Tormented Self

T hree-way love triangles are toxic and destructive and I will never have any part of them at this point in my life. I'm different now.

I think trying to get inside a solid relationship or even making eyes at a man that is not yours, is toxic and deadly to the soul. It causes death and destruction to families. It is not to be messed with under any circumstances.

As part of my healing journey with Coach Dana, I read a book by Debbie Ford, *The Dark Side of the Light Chasers*.

Debbie Ford was a drug addict in her early adult life and she overcame her drug addiction by "embracing her shadow self".

In the book, she talked about the fact that we all have the full spectrum of negative and positive emotions and traits.

By accepting the full continuum of the spectrum, we can have a greater and healthier understanding of ourselves.

There was an exercise in the book where you had to envision yourself at your lowest point, like for me in a men's bathroom sucking a stranger's dick or being a little girl getting molested in exchange for cigarettes, or the Danny Tango episode.

Then I would envision myself at my best, most beautiful, and healthy.

My Best Self and My Worst Self meet in a garden and embrace and comfort each other. We connect, accept, and merge the two selves, which are on a continuum.

I am no different from the crack whore at the train station. It's only by the grace of God that I am at this point in recovery.

This book helped me tremendously when it came to accepting my past shameful experiences as a part of the fabric that now makes me a more solid, emotionally resilient, wise woman.

It also helped me to take responsibility for all my actions and embrace them as a really hard learning experience rather than a series of unfortunate events.

However, the addiction did steal time, energy, and joy from my family and work life and did create some toxic "love" triangles. It really does suck that these things happened. I am sorry to anyone I have hurt. I ignored the ramifications at the time, but today I acknowledge the collateral damage it caused.

More recently, after I declared myself free from sex addiction, a handsome married man was giving me the Sex Eye. I glared back with a determined Sex Eye blocker, clearly communicating the rejection. Progress has been made.

30

Reflections on My Father

I believe that my relationship with my father contributed to my sex and food addiction. I am writing this chapter as an act of forgiveness to my father.

He died when I was 27 years old, but to me, he was dead 8 years prior to that when I shut off my emotions to him. He had broken my heart so many times as a child and teenager, and I was just done with him. I only cried at his funeral with relief that his psychological suffering was over and that I didn't have to deal with him anymore.

My father committed suicide after suffering from psychotic depression. He believed that he had cancer hiding in his abdomen causing debilitating pain, despite going to countless doctors, having numerous scans, and even exploratory abdominal surgeries looking for the source of his pain. He did not have cancer, but feared it so much and felt "cancer pain" to the degree that he decided to take his own life.

My father was a very tormented person. He had ADHD and Tourette's syndrome. I did not learn about what Tourette's Syndrome is until I was in my 20's so as a child, not knowing of a diagnosis, I would just be perplexed by my father's constant jerking and flailing arm spasms, constant muttering, and profane outbursts. His psychotic depression was severe enough to cause him to kill himself with a cocktail of sedative medications and a plastic bag on his head. He was a domestic abuser and overall rage-a-holic. And, come to find out, he had maladaptive sexual behaviors as evidenced by all the women he "cheated" with, the porn magazine collection, and his overall attitude towards objectifying women's bodies. However, I was too young to understand the extent of it, and he too kept much of his behavior secret.

Before the internet existed, kids would find porn magazines that belonged to adults. I found my father's stash of Playboy, Hustler, and Penthouse when I was 8 years old. I was a latchkey child and things were not hidden well anyway.

My father had many amazing qualities. He was highly intelligent and a successful computer programmer. He graduated from the best university in the Soviet Union and brought my mother and me to this beautiful country when I was five years old. He wanted me, his daughter, to have the American Dream.

But the stress of being an immigrant and finding work and building up your finances from nothing takes its toll. And since my father had mental health issues, the stress was manifested in horrible ways.

My father beat my mother and his sister as I witnessed it. Of course, this horrified me, but like most domestic abusers, my father would "apologize" with extended time periods of good behavior and acts of generosity, and I would continue to love him anyway.

My father was always "hot" for pretty women and open with his comments or physicality around women. He was always cheating on my mother, until their divorce when I was 8 years old. I mostly have memories of my mother crying when she was married to my father.

My father contributed to my hyper-sexualization. On one occasion at age 11, I was on a crowded bus, standing and some man was humping me pretending it was the sway of the bus. I only realized when we got off the bus that the man was molesting me. I told my father and he burst out laughing, saying "Oh the guys in this area just like to have a little fun, no big deal." Perhaps he did not know how to respond at that moment, but I was led to believe that I was not protected by the primary man in my life.

When I was 13 years old and in a full-blown new woman's body, my father took us on a vacation to Rio de Janeiro. In Rio, women wear tiny string bikinis barely covering their parts. At that time in the US, only one-piece bathing suits were sold and as a chubby teen with large breasts, I wouldn't be caught dead in a string bikini. My father berated me the entire vacation that I did not buy a string bikini to wear on the Brazilian beach. He said that I looked like a "stupid American" in my one-piece bathing suit. There were countless more body image-type scenarios where my father led me to believe I was just a piece of meat.

I thought that if my father is this way, all men must be crazed, out-of-control sexual beasts. This behavior was normal to me.

I became increasingly estranged from my father until his death. The man I refer to as "my parents" in a previous chapter is my stepfather, my mother's second husband.

When my biological father died, I was completely disinherited. His assets went to my stepmother whom I feel expedited and contributed to his suicide and to the organization, Friends of the Dying, which provided assistance in his suicide. The disinheritance made me "forget" my father even more. He was long dead to me and when he was actually dead, if there is such a thing as "deader", he was.

I have compassion for my father now that I know what mental illness and addiction are, I feel his bad behaviors were just that. It is likely that I similarly traumatized my own children with my own dysfunction.

When I look past the mental illness and addiction, my father was kind, generous, intelligent, hard-working, funny, cheerful... And he loved me.

31

Putting the Pieces Together

I am so grateful to be on this side of recovery. Is it perfect? No, but it's better. The healing journey is not without new cracks in my <u>Kintsugi Vase</u>. I will continue to repair, and that process is lifelong.

In summary, here is how a true recovery unfolded for me. Acknowledging my problem was my first step in disarming it.

I am a sex addict.
I have disordered eating.
I am powerless over this addiction.
I need a power greater than me to overcome this.
"God, please help me with this."

I realized that it's not only okay to surrender to this weakness and illness, it's vital. Only from there, could the next steps be taken to resolve it, conquer it, overcome it, learn from it, and heal from it.

I recommend a qualified one-on-one coach or therapist to work with through this process. The reason that Dana successfully helped me is because she reinforced the spiritual component of healing. This is why anti-depressants or anti-anxiety medications could never accomplish this for me. Talking about past traumas and rehashing everything without a spiritual context, left me in further pain and did not provide any meaningful answers. . The ONLY thing that ultimately helped me heal was putting the traumas, guilt, and events of the past into the perspective of God's greater plan for me and for those I love. What I have determined is that these were all symptoms for a spiritual malady.

I do not consider myself to be religious. I do not attend any house of worship. I do, however, believe in a Higher Power and that there is justice and a reason for everything even if I don't understand "why" at the moment. Dana suggested to me that my son, Alex, and I have a "soul contract" with one another and that my actions did not cause his disability. The concept behind a soul contract is that individuals remain connected throughout as many lifetimes deemed necessary in order to resolve the lessons for each soul (in other words, person). That means there is as much for me to learn in this lifetime as there is for Alex. This spiritual agreement is mutually beneficial even if from the outside it appears unfair, unjust or one-sided. In actuality it is what is required for the ultimate outcome of an enlightened and peaceful soul. Some refer to this as karma. Deciding to see the gifts and lessons in the pain and anguish of a relationship is entirely up to the individual(s) in this lifetime. Considering this new-found perspective, I was then able to release myself from the cycle of punishment from "enjoying" my sex abuse as a child, to causing my son's disability, to punishing myself for having no control as it pertained to acting out on my food and sex addictions. I began to see myself as worthy of a peaceful, content, successful life.

My sex and food addiction had been my escape and my punishment for decades. It is a wonder how the dagger of addiction works in this way.

When I allowed myself to learn from the events of the past, it empowered me. I grew in wisdom from it, and when I was able to share it with a trusted Coach, healing myself and those affected and harmed in its wake felt possible.

The final step for me was to declare that I am free from addiction.
I am no longer a sex addict. I conduct myself like I admire and respect myself. I no longer have disordered eating. I eat like a normal person. I eat, exercise, think, fuck, talk, and act as if I love myself.

Declaring myself free from the addiction does not mean that I am perfect or not susceptible to a fuck up. It means that I am no longer living with the pathological label so that I subconsciously lived "down" to it or have an excuse when I do fuck up. It means I no longer harbor any expectation of living in the experience of that addiction label or cycle.

Furthermore, I certainly don't ever want to live with regret, that is why I say I take complete responsibility and ownership of my actions.

I often think, if I didn't have a sex addiction, I could've done everything better. I would have had more time and energy for my kids, my spouse, my work, and for my overall health.

However, in Gabor Maté's book, he states, "There is nothing lost," meaning the gifts of the spiritual quest compensate for the shit that happened in the past.

In one of Coach Dana's Mindset Modules, she assigned an exercise to write "My Own Success Story". It was an exercise very early in the Mindset course that made me articulate what my goals were. The following letter was dated February 2, 2022. When I wrote it, I was in the depths of despair, praying for healing. One year later, every word of this letter was true. Here it is:

"I am amazed at how food is neutral to me. I choose to fuel my body in just the right portion that I need. I am able to enjoy the taste and not feel like I need to eat an enormous amount. I am so happy that I have a great relationship with Richard and the kids. I live in love that everything happens for a reason and events are inter-connected. There IS justice in the Universe. I am at peace with myself and the traumas of the past have been given meaning and are now contributing constructively to my life. I am a stronger, more vibrant person because I feel my emotions, share my joys, and I communicate my feelings as needed. I celebrate my success and how I have grown emotionally and spiritually. I marvel at how accomplished I am in my life and all the chapters that I have endured. My wisdom and radiant soul spills over into everyone I meet and I am able to help them with their problems and perceptions. I finally have inner peace. I finally have inner peace."

32

Repairing the Damage

Richard has forgiven me and we are still together. But, of course, he has not forgotten. I will be making amends to him for the rest of my life. His trust was repeatedly betrayed by me and that has certainly made him more jaded over time and has changed his personality somewhat, to be less jovial and carefree.

How does one make amends for repeated betrayals?

I make it my daily practice to hug and kiss, and tell Richard that I love him every morning and every night and whenever possible in between. I still apologize to him for the same things I have apologized for many times. He just absorbs my words and mostly stays silent when I apologize for the past. I want him to know that I too will never forget the pain that I caused and how tremendously appreciative I am for our relationship surviving.

Love is an action. I follow the "Five Love Languages" to make amends. I show my love with physical affection, "hold my hand." I show my love with words of affirmation, "You are the most handsome man ever!" I show my love with acts of service, " I cleaned the bathroom today." And, "Here's a sandwich I made for lunch." I show my love with gifts, "I thought this shirt would look great on you!." I show my love by spending quality time, "Let's go for a hike together." Richard appreciates acts of service and words of affirmation the most, so I focus more on these.

The more time that passes, I am more appreciative, more respectful of his inner strength, and much more in love with Richard.

I will continue to make amends to Richard forever. I want him to trust me. I think the trust factor for Richard is still very frail and fragile. I hope it will continue to strengthen over time.

I acknowledge the hurt and pain that I have caused Richard's daughter and his brothers, who also knew of some of our relationship problems. There was a tremendous ripple effect of the damage that my sex addiction caused. I am working to make amends for this for the rest of my life.

If my family, husband, and acquaintances ever read this book, my hope is that they have empathy for me; That they will gain insight into my shadows, forgive me, and still love me.

My three beautiful children– I love you. I am sorry if I caused you emotional trauma. I did the best I could under my circumstances. I am proud of you and pray that you don't have any of the dysfunction that ran in our family.

Dear Richard- I believe in Divine Intervention and you were the angel sent to keep me safe. I am sure of that. I will love you forever.

If you enjoyed this book, please leave a favorable review where you purchased this book or any social media platform. It helps tremendously with spreading the message of this book and its success. If you would like to correspond with me directly please email me at ppanties333@gmail.com I would love to hear from my readers.

Afterword

By Dana Lee Chapman

Although I am a specialist who helps women heal from decades of dieting and food dysfunction, it is undeniable that one's addiction to food can often run parallel to their addiction to sex.

As Paulina shares in Part One of this book, the term "sex addiction" is misleading. I agree with her for similar reasons that "food addiction" is not accurate.

It's not the sex itself. It's not the food itself.

The addiction exists and is fed (I guess you could say) by the innermost desires to find love, connection, nourishment and escape the heavy burden of shame. Addiction is then further fueled as a means to punish oneself for 1) The initial incident(s) that caused the desire to escape life in the first place and 2) Acting on a compulsion even when you logically know it's harmful behavior, yet you do it anyway.

Although there may have been a cause for the addiction to begin in the first place, punishment is the fuel that keeps it going.

This is why shaming the behavior is never going to be the way the behavior is ultimately healed. Feeling ashamed about the binge only makes you binge more. Feeling embarrassed of the sex only makes you want more sex with someone who doesn't know your deep, dark secrets. It can be filed under the category of "why bother changing" and "I'm a bad person at the core." Neither of which are actually True. They are thoughts and beliefs. Therefore, breaking the destructive patterns can only happen when the need to punish oneself is removed from the equation.

It must be acknowledged that food and sex are two addictions that are challenging to overcome because of our need to eat food to live and have sex as part of our biology to procreate and keep the human race alive. That craving and desire is strong to begin with because of basic survival.

It is absolutely possible for Paulina to have been "addicted to" donuts for years, then after doing the inner work on re-learning what it's like to love and respect herself (no longer having the desire to punish herself), she could either have a bite of a donut and leave it, or decide that she isn't interested in donuts anymore because she up-leveled her appreciation for food and is more discerning about what she puts in, and how she treats, her body. She decided to raise the standard and set boundaries for herself, which means that food is no longer something she has a desire to manipulate and abuse anymore.

The same goes for sex. It is possible to re-learn healthy intimacy and appreciate and experience sex in a whole new way when you are more discerning with how you treat your body and what you put in your body. Again - standards and boundaries that come from within.

A healthy relationship with food and with sex is the side-effect from having more love, respect and care for who you are and what you have been through rather than looking at it through condemning eyes. You already tried that approach and it's proven to be unhelpful and only the cause of more pain and anguish.

How does one reconcile with abusing and over-dosing on the very things that are part of our survival?

This book has a lot of those answers if you read between the lines and contemplate the somewhat rhetorical questions that Paulina poses for you at the end of each chapter. Take the time to reflect upon them, just like she had done for herself, and see what you learn about yourself.

Something pretty spectacular happens when you muster up the courage to look at the hidden parts of yourself that you have demonized and hated, felt shameful and embarrassed about for much of your life. Writing your thoughts in a journal is a good first step to figuring things out.

When you are ready to share these things verbally with someone you trust and who has demonstrated their capacity to be an emotionally intelligent and competent human you feel safe with (this is where a trained trauma therapist or coach is recommended), in that secret telling, more love, respect and honor can be restored within yourself.

It's like a pressure cooker. Emotional pain has been building up tension and pressure inside you for years, having no new or healthy outlet, nowhere to go. This can be the reason why you may feel ailments, pains and aches in your physical body manifesting itself, as Paulina correlated with her own story regarding cancer. When you release the fear and pressure of judgment and shunning by talking about it honestly, the reward is that it creates an opening for ease, peace, calm, and acceptance to be allowed in its place.

Paulina was fortunate to have such a patient, loving, and understanding long-term partner in Richard. He was gifted with the ability to see his wife for who she really was, beneath the addictions. He also had a desire to learn as much as possible about sex addiction so that he could be the supportive force to help assist her on her own path to recovery. After all, he was the one who confronted her with the thought of "sex addiction" in the first place. He took on a very different role than an "enabling" one in her life.

There were times Richard left, and then decided to return. This makes the case for why it's so important to develop boundary setting as a skill. Boundary-setting is not the same as giving an ultimatum. A boundary is a standard you declare for yourself, regardless of whether or not the other party will rise up to meet you. True, it gives them an opportunity to do so, but either way, it's for the well-being of all involved. This is what makes it one of the most challenging things to establish in a relationship affected by addiction. You can love someone deeply and choose to stay. You can love someone deeply and choose to create distance between you. Neither is right or wrong.

It is all a part of your own individual recovery, whether you are the one with the addiction or you are the one who has a relationship with someone who is addicted. There are many nuances to establishing healthy boundaries and the sooner that is acknowledged, the more patience, compassion, and breathing room for the overall process can be experienced.

As Paulina discovered, speaking your truth will set you free. Looking at it piece by piece, taking personal responsibility for your part, deciding to learn both the human and the spiritual lessons while embracing the greatest compassion for yourself along the way are the keys that will unlock the depth of healing from addiction.

Good news: If you were part of creating so many problems in your life, you are also part of creating so many solutions - although never again without spirit/God/Universe by your side. Saying and feeling the Truth of the words "God is with me" will help restore the energy, power and meaning back into your life to the degree that you are open and ready for the spiritual component.

Today is the youngest you will ever be, and also the wisest you've ever been. You are exactly where you need to be and you are ready for the next step.

If you are seeking to connect with me to help facilitate your dysfunctional relationship with food and/or sex, visit my website www.RealFit.tv/talk and fill out the Mindset Questionnaire to see if the method I took Paulina through can help you too.